Dreams & Nightmares from a Daydreamer

Mariana Molina-Lopez

BookLeaf Publishing

India | USA | UK

Dreams & Nightmares from a Daydreamer
© 2024 Mariana Molina-Lopez

All rights reserved.

Mariana Molina-Lopez asserts the moral
right to be identified as the author of this
work.

Presentation by *BookLeaf Publishing*

Web: www.bookleafpub.com

E-mail: info@bookleafpub.com

ISBN: 9789360946104

First edition 2024

To my sunshine boy with stormy eyes.

ACKNOWLEDGEMENT

I want to thank my close group of friends that really believed in me and pushed me to do this challenge and most importantly to finally get serious about my writing. I never would have thought my silly little ideas and poems were good enough or interesting enough to catch anyone's attention. I want to give a really big thanks to Angel who bounced ideas with me and helped me create the vision for this book. I also want to thank my muse who supported me every step on the way. I wouldn't have finished without you.

Most importantly I want to thank all the daydreamers out there. Hopefully these poems make you feel seen and heard.

PREFACE

I always had a passion for writing but it really wasn't until I found my muse that I really dove deep. I wrote like never before and soon this idea of duality flourished. Day and night, dark and light. Which is how I came up with the concept of this book and what better way to incorporate myself than the nickname I've had since I was a child... Daydreamer.

Daydreamer

My love… why the long face…

Are you remembering a time long before ours?
Where your imagination could run free in
visions of an ancient time?
Where kings and queens ruled lands, mystical
beings wandered the earth with mortals.
Are you imagining yourself now in those lands
away from the hard cruelties of the world?

Are you a princess or perhaps a queen?

No, you are too precious, too powerful for such
a weak word.

You must have been a goddess or a high lady of
the Fae.
Were you dancing the night away in a gown as
dark as night but with thousands of stars making
it glimmer under the moonlight?

Are you happy there my beloved?

Don't worry… You run.

Run away to those mystical lands beyond my
comprehension.

I will protect you.

I will take care of you so that you can visit those
grand lands where magick flows through the
ground, casting mountainous trees with power
and energy.
The type that is always buzzing just below the
skin.

Some people might say it's all fake.

That it's all in your mind.

Don't let them sway you darling for you are not
from this mundane world.

You are destined for much more.

You Awaken Me

My love, you awaken me.

You have awoken the desire in me.
And I don't mean sexual desire.
This desire that has awakened in me is much
deeper than something as simple as physical
needs.

You have awakened the desire to want to live.
Not just survive.

To see the world in all its shades and colors, not
just black and white.
To hope for a future that promises better days
and sunny skies, rather than the roar of thunder
and the crack of lightning. Flooding everything
in its wake.
Rather than just trying to survive the day.

You have awakened the desire to create.
To express myself in ways that create these
timeless words that capture every fiber of my
being.
You awaken me in ways that make me feel like
I've been asleep and trapped in a horrible
nightmare for centuries.
But now…

I'm awake.

Not only awake, but with a raging heart that is
no longer locked behind bars with wires and
pins encapsulating it to protect it.
You have removed all those barriers and let me
love you.
These desires to live,
To write,
To paint,
To dance,
To sing.

They were all hidden deep inside.
Devoured by the darkness that swirls endlessly.
Yet you freed those desires.
You freed me.

My love you have awakened me and I never
want to go back to sleep.

I'd Never Thought I'd Write Again

I never thought I'd write again…

Who knew all it takes is one soul who changes it all.

It's always when I talk about how you make me feel that I can't help but paint a beautiful picture with words that describe the vastness and almost clandestine emotions you stir in me.

It's like the world has become anew.
All these new emotions that feel so familiar, yet so foreign.
My mind can't comprehend them, but my heart recognizes them.
My heart knows what they are.
They recognize those deep feelings of our love from a distant past.

So beautiful.
So pure.

It makes me want to write until my hands break and not a single idea is left swirling in my mind.

Until every ounce of my soul has been immortalized in the pages of what I write.

I'd never thought I'd write again but thanks to you… I can…

I'm free.

You Make Me Want to Write Again

You make me want to write about the way the
sun shines brighter and the days are warmer,
Even in the dead of winter.
Since I met you.

You make me want to write about how my heart
races and my mind refuses to shut off at the end
of the night until I talk to you.
To hear your voice.

It's like a trance.
I can't stop the words flowing from my mind.
Each stroke of ink putting into words what I feel
deep in my soul.

You make me want to write again…
Because I believe in love again.

Summer Day Boy

I never cared for blue eyes.

I wasn't like other girls,
As cliché as that sounds,
That daydreamed about a blue-eyed boy with a
sunshine smile.

Yet here I find myself,
Unable to look away from the eyes that reflect
the color of the waters surrounding you.
Those beautiful blue eyes like the depths of the
crystal clear blue Hawaiian waters.
The waters you call home.

I want to dive in and never resurface.

To have those eyes and attention only on me.

To have you never look away.

But your eyes aren't always the clear blue that
everyone says comes with blue eyes.
No.
Some days they're the clear, sunny sky of a
warm summer day,

But some days they're clouded over…
Darker like a storm rampaging the ocean waves.
Threatening to pull me under, until the last
breath has escaped my lungs,
Yet I love them all the same.

So yeah… I never did care for blue eyes…

Until you…

My **Summer Day Boy**.

If I'm Fall You're My Spring Lover

If I remind you of fall,
You are my bright summer day.

If I am the slight chill in the air that has you
reaching for a sweater,
The epitome of cozy comfort.
You are the light breeze at the first sights of
spring that promises endless days of joy and
contentment.

If I'm like a fall day…
You
My spring beloved,
Are the lasting bits of warmth that cling to me
before the harsh winter.

The seasons change like a cycle.
Just like our lives.
But,
What doesn't change, is that the cycle will never
end.

Like our love

Storyteller Eyes

Do you know my love, your eyes tell stories.

But not just any stories.

Prophecies.

When I look into your eyes it's like looking into
the depths of the cerulean blue pools.
Those that reveal the secrets of the universe.

In your eyes, I see a future.
One where children's laughter comes carefree
and fills our days.
Where even on the harsh cold winter nights, our
home is still warm with our love.

My love,
Your eyes tell of a future worth fighting for.

That no matter what challenges threaten to
destroy the very foundation of the fortress that is
our safe haven, with hurtful words or deception,
We will overcome it with understanding and
compassion.
In your eyes,

I see a love that never fades,

Never dies.

A love where even poets can't help but weep at
the sight of such pure, unadulterated love.
A love that transcends any and all lifetimes.

My love,
You have storyteller eyes.

And I want to read every line over and over
again.

Immortal

I want to immortalize you in the pages of my poetry.

To live on even after our mortal bodies have left this existence.

That way, anyone who ever reads these poems can feel your soul.

Remember you even though they never met you.
Your soul would live on in the words I wrote,
On the pages that are no longer blank,
But filled with your bright warm light.

No longer will you fear death or not being
remembered because my love…
You are worth remembering for generations to
come.

Your heart and soul, too grand to be left as a
whisper in time.
In this vast universe.
Much more than a tiny lifetime in the grand
scheme of things.

No, my love… you will be…

Immortal

I Can't Write About Me

I can't write about me because every waking
moment my heart and mind fight over you.

The **Sunshine Boy** to the darkness of my moon.
The ray of light in the vastness of my
all-consuming night.

How easily you fill my thoughts with ideas and
visions I want to paint with words.
My poems are just words on paper,
But it is you who brings them alive.

You and your **Storyteller Eyes**

The soul I want to **Immortalize** in my writing

I can't write about me, when the desire to inspire
you creeps into my consciousness.
When I secretly hope that my poems inspire
your creative mind like you inspire mine.

That's why I can't write about me.
But I could spend an eternity happily writing
about you.

Learn How to Read

I want you to learn how to read.

And that's not me calling you illiterate.

The type of reading I want you to learn is not
from any book or any tale.
I want you to learn how to read me.

How to read my soul.

It's not just the physical body language, or the
way I give you looks.

It's about noticing the little details. Like when I
start to fidget when I get anxious,
Or notice how my eyes brighten when I see a
beautiful scene or see something I love.

The way I lose myself in my daydreams. When
my eyes are casted over like the misty ocean
and my mind is far away.

I want you to learn how to read my soul.

Like an open book, where you devour the pages
of every chapter of my life.
The good
The bad
The moments where I didn't think I could go on.

To read and study each line of my soul like your
life depended on it.
Until you know every detail of who I am,
Where I've been,
And why I am the way I am.

And once you're done, I only ask for one thing…

For you to still love me anyways…

To be known is to be loved.

So please… Learn how to read so you can truly know me.

Always the Poet, Never the Muse

I never believed myself good enough to have
such beautiful words
That paint the skies and daydreams to be about
me.

Such a foreign concept.

The idea that someone like me could inspire a
beautiful poet, writer, or composer to create
beauty from the darkness within.

It is unfathomable.

To have someone like me who bears their heart
and soul in these words that change your view of
everything you know.
The image of someone slaving over a desk
trying to formulate and put together the most
enchanting and entrancing words, to capture the
simple essence of my soul and being.
To immortalize me in those pages or songs.

I could never imagine it.

I am always the poet and never the muse…
But yet…

You have made me your muse.

You have taken my essence and captured it into
your own precious words.
The melodies that play from your heart create a
symphony, that paints promises of a better
future.
One full of smiles and laughter that I crave so
dearly.

You have made me your muse.

To live on forever in your mind and soul.
But also in the words you speak.
The poetry you write.
The music you make.

I was always the poet but now…

I'm your muse.

I Would Find You in Every Lifetime

I would find you in every lifetime.
My heart and soul would recognize you in any
body.
Anywhere.

Your laugh that feels like a warm summer
breeze,
That brightens my days.

Ending my everlasting night.

Your voice that makes me want to stop and
listen.
To hang onto every word you say like my life
depends on it.
Your mind that inspires me to create,
To hope,
To wish,
To dream.

I'd recognize you in every lifetime because my
soul recognizes yours.
It recognizes the feeling of home.

The feeling of you.

Soulmates is too mundane of a term for how my
soul radiates in tandem with yours.
We could be miles apart,
An ocean between us,
And yet I would still find you.

Like Achilles and Patroclus,
Our love and bond transcends the Gods'
themselves.

Like Orpheus and Eurydice,

I would go to the depths of the Underworld to
plead for you back.
Even if it meant trading your soul for mine.

Like Psyche and Eros,
I would always find a way back to you,
No matter the trials and tribulations that tried to
keep us apart.

My love,
I would find you in every lifetime,
Because I have found you in every lifetime
and…

I will always find you.

Breathe

Breathe.

Just one breath at a time.

But how am I supposed to breathe, when you make me feel like the world is shattering under me.
Your lips on my skin, sending electric shocks through my spine down to my core.
Your hands exploring my body with a desperation.
Like you need to learn every inch,
Every Curve,
To survive.

Breathe,
You tell me.

But how am I supposed to breathe when the
flames of our desire have suffocated the room of
all oxygen.
When our desires have made us succumb to the
pure and untainted,
Almost primal,
Need within us.

Breathe.

But how can I do that when you fill me up until I
can't take any more.
Until you spread me open like a book.
Letting all your fantasies and desires come out
of the pages.
When I feel your lips on my neck.

Can you feel my heart racing for you?

Just breathe you say…

Yet if I took my last breath right now, there
would be not a single regret in my soul.

Russian Roulette with Your Lover

Do you want to play this game?

To risk your life with mine?

"What's life without a little risk?" You respond.

My dear… You don't know.

You don't know the darkness underneath, that
makes my mind wander to all these dark desires.
That have us tethering with our lives on the line.
I'm ok with putting the bullet through my brain.

I can feel it now.

The cold metal grazing the insides of the black
caverns between my ears.

But you my love…

I refuse to let you play this risk.
Your life is too precious…
To warm with summer rays.

My dear, don't play this game…

I can't control fate.

I Will Never Question if I am Good Enough

I will never question if I am good enough,

Because of the way you looked at me.

You looked at me like I was the sun, moon, and stars.
When in reality I am the darkness that encompasses it all.

I will never question if I am good enough again.

Because of the way you checked on me like no one has before.
The way you check on me when I've been in the shower too long, because you know those treacherous thoughts slither into my mind.
Threatening to drown me in those same waters pouring down on me.
The way you text me 3 times a day,
Asking if I have eaten, because you know of that dark time in my past when I couldn't even take a bite.

I will never question if I am good enough again.

Because even though I had lost you..
Which I still don't understand why it got that far.

I was able to see myself through your eyes and see the beauty I had hidden from myself.
Shamed myself into believing that I didn't have the beauty I yearned for.

I will never question if I am good enough again.

Because you taught me…
I am good enough
I am more than that.

I am a Goddess.

Nightmares

TRIGGER WARNING:
THE NIGHTMARE POEMS CONTAIN HEAVY TOPICS
(I.E. SUICIDE, SA, ETC) THAT CAN BE DISTURBING
AND UPSETTING. READERS DISCRETION IS ADVISED.

REMEMBER YOUR MENTAL HEALTH MATTERS ♥

Nightmares

My mind works in mysterious ways that even I cannot seem to comprehend.

Some days it creates beautiful images that have me racing towards my pen to paint the beautiful imagery in my mind with words and ink.

Yet most days it feels like an unknown,
neverending cavern with no light in sight.

Sometimes, I wonder if others truly love me or
is it all just a facade?
One last trick before leaving me alone in the
dark.
Sometimes, I wonder if life is worth living.
If there is more to this sometimes meaningless
existence.

My mind twists and turns with the thought of the
macabre. Thoughts of death or thereafter. How
easy it would be to just take one more pill, one
more slash, or merely one more step into
oncoming traffic.

The thoughts come out of nowhere. They turn
my daydreams into nightmares.
My greatest fears plaguing my mind relentlessly.
Demanding space in my subconscious.
It turns roses into deadly nightshade, puppies
into flesh-eating beasts, and those I love into
corpses beneath my feet.

Sometimes, I wonder if there's something wrong
with me but then I remember…

You have to be a little mad to be a poet.

Daydreamer Pt.2

Sometimes being a daydreamer isn't all that it's cut out to be…

Yes, you get to dream up these lavish fantasies and escape the harsh realities of the world.
But also, you lose touch with reality and that is one of the dangers no one talks about.
No one warns you about it.

You forget about the time that passes.
It happens slowly.

You don't realize it until it's too late.

You have completely lost touch with the world
around you.
You lost contact with those you care about.
Life events flashed before your eyes and you
didn't even bat an eye because for you, a second
has yet to pass by.

One moment you are just succumbing and
fading into the sweet bliss that is slipping into a
daydream.
Feeling the world around you fade slowly,
transitioning to the wonderful daydream.
Then next thing you know,

POOF

You're back in the real world and days have
gone by since you last communicated with
anyone…and people get tired of it.

You lose those you love because they don't
believe they're important to you.
You beg and cry that it won't happen again but
they don't believe you.

They refuse to believe you can change.
They truly believe that your little world doesn't
include them.

So yeah… being a daydreamer isn't always
everything it's cut out to be.

A Poet in a Fast Moving World

I'm just a hopeless romantic in a world where
life moves too quickly.
It fades attraction into boredom.
It fades the sparks of love into nothing but
embers.
A fire once lit that burned bright, snuffing out
under the constraints of a fleeting moment.
The wondrous emotions flowing inside me,
dissipating as soon as they come.

It's tiring.

One second you feel all the love in the world.
The beauty of all realms, to then,

Nothing.

Everything is fleeting, yet something about that
too is beautiful.
It brings out the urge to capture that moment,
both physically and mentally before it can
disappear.

The rush of scrambling to put the words on paper, or type out the emotions or visions in my mind…

All fleeting…
Yet for that one second, it is all vividly real.

I guess I'm just a poet in a fast moving world.

Invincible

With you by my side nothing can go wrong.

You are my strength and my kryptonite all at the
same time.
You raise me up but bring me to my knees.

I thought I was strong before you but this new
strength… I could take on the world.
I'd burn the world if any disrespect came your
way.

You're my salvation and damnation all at once.

It's like I can breathe again, yet I'm drowning.
I am untouchable, yet a touch from you melts
me into nothing.

You are my shield and the knife in my ribs.

These feelings are beautiful like a summer day
but also chaotic and dangerous like
thunderstorms with flooding rain.

But when you ice me out…
When you no longer deem me worthy of your
love, it feels like a winter storm.

The ice, freezing over my heart.
Everything is dull and dead and I can't see a
future beyond these dark few hours.

Why must I crave your approval so mother…
Isn't a mother's love supposed to be
unconditional?

Should I feel…invincible?

Guilt & Greed

"Why must money make the world go around?"

"Because people made it that way my love."

Greed overruns love and respect.
People only think of the next cash grab.

The next opportunity to climb that corporate
ladder just to increase their greed.

The money we make brings wealth.
Wealth brings power and influence.

Why does it matter in this game we call life?

Passions are burned out in exchange for a viable
future.
Time is lost away from those you love in
exchange for a couple of extra dollars.

At the end of your life, will chasing that paper
even be worth it if it means the total loss of who
you are?

NO!

(A big thank you to Angel for helping me put this concept into motion and inspiring me to dig deep for this one.)

Such a simple word that so many don't seem to
understand. No matter the context.

"No, I'm scared."
But no one listens to the fears that shake you to
your bare bones.
The type of fear that fills every fiber of your
being with the urge to run… run far away.
Chalking it up to your childish fears when you
sense something ominous lurking in the
shadows.
Something that makes your stomach churn and
disturbs you to your core.

But no…
You're just being silly.

"No, I don't want to."
But that plea falls on deaf ears when unwanted
hands touch and taint the most precious and
intimate parts of you.
Those tender parts that only a partner should
have the privilege to feel, to touch, to adore.
Yet their filthy hands don't stop.
No matter the tears streaming down your cheeks
and staining your face.
Or the silent screams you hold back.

But no…

You're just being difficult.

No…
2 letters
1 sound

A word full of power, but powerless when heard
by ignorant fools.

I Want to Go Home

But I don't mean the home where I am
now…no…
My humble apartment in this city, where I was
born and raised is no home to me now.
These four walls, adorned with lights, altars, and
paintings hold nothing but emptiness in them.

It's not because I don't like this place or because
it's small and old.
It's because it's missing a crucial thing.

It's missing you…

You, who inspired so many ideas that swirl in
my mind day and night. You, who has made me

smile my days away even when I thought I
wouldn't be able to get out of this nightmare.
You, who made the days brighter and the nights
warmer.

Just… you…

People say home is where the heart is…

Well for me my heart ... My home is
2,716 miles away.
3 states over.
5h nonstop flight.

So yes, I will spill tears and throw a fit like an
upset child because you are my home, and I can't
come home every night.
That's why everyday I'll keep repeating it until
the words sound like they're coming from a
broken record that can only play the same
melancholy tune.
It just repeats…

I want to go home.

Slashes and Cuts

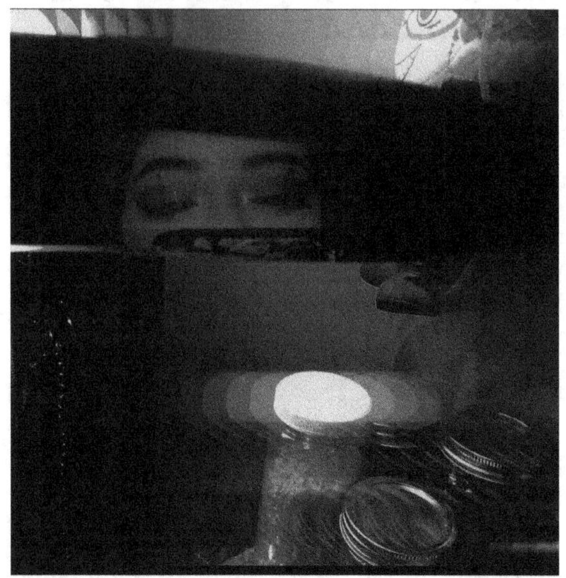

Slashes and cuts.

It's not the type that you think.

It's not the ones on our skin buried under
repressed memories.
No
These cuts are worse…

They hurt deeper.

They hurt the soul.
Because they aren't caused by external pains of
others' words.
Or even the harsh cruelties of the world.
They are caused by the unyielding desire to want
to talk to you…

To hear your voice but being unable to.

They hurt deep my love.

They bleed deeper too..

Aching

That is what my heart is doing right now.

Aching.

Such an unbearable pain that I couldn't describe
it even if I tried.
The worst of all is that the wound causing the
pain is invisible.

No one but me can see the dagger in my heart.
Penetrating it deep from my back because of the
betrayal.

Yet you see this level of pain is only the first
stage.
When the wound is still fresh.
I still feel the dagger lodged in my heart.
I could see the garnets like the ring you
promised me on the handle gleam.
The red beautiful stones, the same shade as my
broken heart.

Nonetheless that is not the worst part.

The aching…

The aching feeling when I am reminded that
you're not here.
The ache in my heart after I forget for a second
that you have left me and I still try to call you on
my break.
Or call you when I'm off because you always
wanted to make sure I got home safe.
The aching I feel when someone uses one of
your phrases,
Knowing that I will never hear it from you
again.

It's like you're holding my heart in your hands
and slowly
Painfully slow…
Applying pressure, squeezing my heart as my
blood gushes down your arm like water.
What's worst of all is that the aching never truly
goes away.
It always comes back when you least expect it.

Yes I am aching…constantly aching…
But you know what they say…

Time heals all.

Empty

Empty…

Some days I just feel empty.
But it's not the emptiness that wretches your
heart out after aching all day.
It's not the emptiness that comes after the loss of
something or someone.
This emptiness is like a shadow that suddenly
surrounds you in a world of grey…
Not even the all-consuming darkness of black
but…

Just grey.

There's nothing to feel and worst of all,
It hits randomly and without a care of who
you're with or where you are.

It creates a storm in my mind with words and
ideas that I can't catch or capture in their
fleeting moments.
Thought after thought racing in my mind, yet in
my heart there's nothing.
My heart feels nothing.
Like an uninspired writer with pens full of ink
but pages stark white with nothing…

Just Emptiness.

It's worse than feeling pain.
At least with pain you feel something
You know you are alive.

As I lay here on the cold tile floor, letting the
emptiness caress and devour my soul I
wonder…

Am I alive?

Will I ever feel again?

The Bath is Dangerous

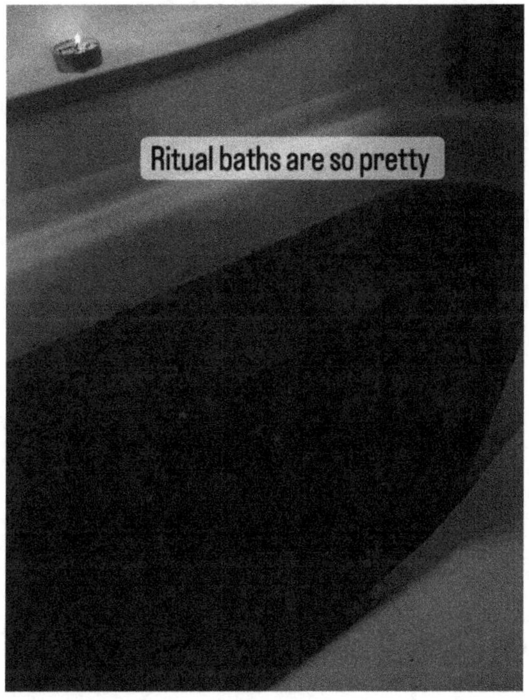

The bath is dangerous darling.
It gives you a false sense of comfort and
relaxation when you're in it.
When truly it's hiding deadly secrets underneath.

The warmth of the water and the scent of the
candle slowly relaxing each tense, aching
muscle in your body.
Giving you a false sense of security as it fails to
relax the one muscle that is in most pain.

The mind.

My mind spins and swirls with all thoughts.
Some of pure nature but most of darkness.
Thoughts that I only let myself succumb to in
the lull of the slight movement of the water in
the bathtub.

I take one long breath.

Letting the scent of the candle fill my lungs as I
give in to the dark desires.
Under the water I hear my heart racing, then
steadying, then racing again against my instincts'
desire for air.
As I shut my eyes and see the flash of those
clear blue eyes turn into a storm of darkness.
I let go of the last breath in my lungs.
Like how you let go and snuffed out the candle
of our love with one question in the air…

Why?

Savior?

You were the Hercules to my Meg.
I knew you were either going to save my soul or
curse it for all eternity.
The hope of saving me from drowning in the
deep dark waters of the river Styx.
Or you would leave me, condemning me to the
bitter cold waters of the Underworld.

You were the Hades to my Persephone
You used to inspire me to revel in my darker
desires.
To accept that darkness that lay dormant inside
me.
Yet you robbed the spring from my lungs and
dragged me under deeper than I dare go.

Like Orpheus, you looked back too soon,
Let me go too soon.
Now here I am.
Back in the darkness with no hope of seeing the
light again.
The light that shined in your crystal blue eyes
and sunshine smile.
It was stripped away leaving nothing but stormy
eyes and a coldness in my blood.

A coldness that feels like frost has invaded that
red stream.

You were Michael and I was Lucifer.
You could have saved my soul,
But instead you damned me to the depths of hell.
Now, I am a fallen angel, doomed forever with
betrayal in my eyes and a sadness in my heart.

You could have been my hero…my savior.

So why wasn't I worth saving?

Shattered

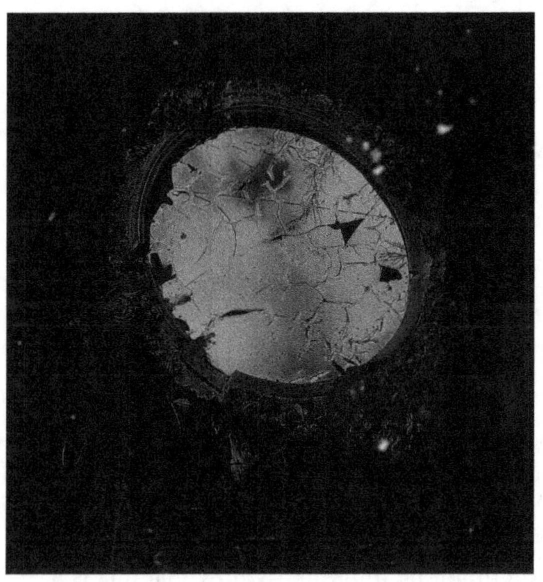

Creak…Break…Shatter

Sometimes that's what happens with your heart
It shatters like glass,
Those sharp shards inside,
Tearing everything around in your soul and
consciousness.
It hurts and it aches.

An unbearable pain

where it seems like the pain itself has stolen the
very air you need to
Breathe.

A pressure unlike any other.
Like one that would collapse mountains
And drain the sea.

Those shards hurt,
But they do more than hurt.
They bleed.

The bleeding starting to drip into the vast hole
created in your chest,
That slowly starts healing into nothingness.
An echo of what it used to be.

You might be thinking by now that this is a
heartbreak poem but this is where the twist
comes in…

Sometimes that ache and pain can be dulled by
soft reassurance.
Kind words…
Kind eyes…
The promise of patience and compromise
by the one that shattered it in the first place.

Some might call me a fool for believing
something like this.
That the person who shattered your heart can't
heal or mend it.
That it's all a lie.
It may well be just that, but you'll never know
unless you try.

Love isn't just about the excitement, or the
feeling of love, or heartbreak but it's also about
the journey taken,

And the forgiveness used.

I'm Sorry

I'm sorry you were hurting and I couldn't see it.
I was too blinded by your sunshine smile
To see the storms creeping into your ocean blue
eyes.

I'm sorry you had to choose between our love
and your best friend,
Because I was too scared and couldn't let go of
the past.

I'm sorry you had to go through unwanted
touches,
When they couldn't take no for an answer.
For a boss who abused his power and position.

I'm sorry you were alone in the moments you
needed someone at your side.

I'm sorry for ignoring the pain that the decision
you made had on you.
So upset.
So angry.
I couldn't see that it hurt and broke your heart
too.

I'm sorry you felt so alone.

I'm sorry to my **Sunshine Boy**.

To My Sunshine Boy with Stormy Eyes

I hope you are happy now. I truly mean it.

I hope you find the love you always wanted,
Like the love we always talked about.

A future that promises those bright sunny days
filled with happiness.

I hope you have found your muse again, who
inspires you to create light beautiful pieces and
shoot for the stars.

I would have never known truly why you left.
Why you had betrayed me like that.

To rip the sunshine away only leaving stormy
dark skies.
Skies that cried just like me until I couldn't
differentiate the skies' tears from mine.

I had somehow become the villain in your story
in less than an hour.
That's all it took…
But you know what…

If I had to be the villain in your story during that
time to keep inspiring you,
To keep being your dark muse, then that's what I
was willing to become.
I would be your dark queen of nightmares to
inspire your writing,
Your music.
You.

So to my sunshine boy with stormy eyes, I just
hope that one day those eyes turn clear blue
again...now that you are by my side once again
<3